# GREAT APES

**Max Fax:**

# GREAT APES

Also in this series:
*Aircraft*
*Big Cats*
*Cars*
*Sharks*
*Space*

Cover photograph: Face to face with a Lowlands gorilla

**Commissioning editor:** Lisa Edwards
**Series editor:** Cath Senker
**Designer:** Luke Herriott
**Illustrator:** Mike Atkinson
**Researchers:** Gina Brown and Shelley Noronha
**Language consultant:** Wendy Cooling
**Subject consultant:** Stephen Savage

First published in Great Britain in 2001
by Hodder Wayland, an imprint of
Hodder Children's Books
This paperback edition published in 2001

© Copyright 2001 Hodder Wayland

British Library Cataloguing in Publication Data
Llewellyn, Claire
Great Apes. – (Max fax)
1. Apes – Juvenile literature
I. Title
599.8'8
ISBN: 0 7502 34229

Printed in Hong Kong

Hodder Children's Books
A division of Hodder Headline Limited
338 Euston Road, London NW1 3BH

# GREAT APES

Claire Llewellyn

HODDER
*Wayland*

*an imprint of Hodder Children's Books*

# CONTENTS

LOOKING AT APES      8

AN APE'S BODY      10

SWINGING ALONG      12

A GORILLA'S DAY      14

AMBUSH!      16

BRAINY APES      18

BABY APE      20

APES IN DANGER      22

HELPING APES      24

APES QUIZ      26

GLOSSARY      28

FINDING OUT MORE      29

INDEX      30

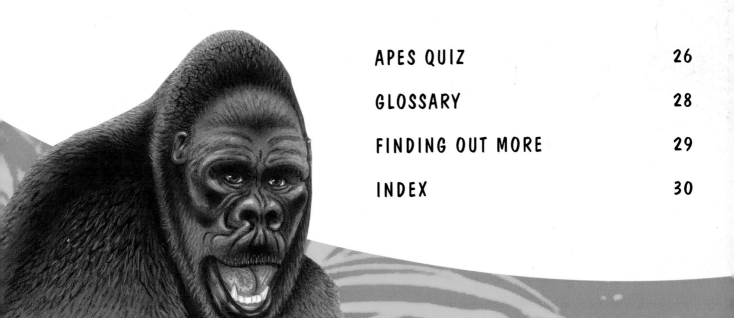

# LOOKING AT APES

Apes are a small family of animals. They are not beautiful, or fierce. So why do we find them so interesting? Is it because apes are our closest relatives, and remind us of ourselves?

*The orang-utan lives deep in tropical forests.*

*Gorillas are the largest apes. This is a mountain gorilla.*

**There are five** different kinds of ape. The gorilla, orang-utan, chimpanzee and bonobo are called the great apes. The gibbon is called a lesser ape because it is so small.

**Apes belong** to an animal group called the primates. Primates have eyes that face forwards and a thumb that swivels. Primates can also stand upright, at least for a while.

Apes live where it's warm. Gibbons and orang-utans live in the steamy rainforests of south-east Asia. Gorillas, chimps and bonobos live in Africa – in grasslands, woods or thick mountain forests.

Different apes have different lifestyles. Chimps and bonobos live in large groups of up to 100; gorillas live in groups of between five and twenty; gibbons live as couples, and orang-utans live all alone.

## Which other animals are primates?

Monkeys, bushbabies, lemurs and humans.

## Are apes different from monkeys?

Yes. Apes are larger, more intelligent, and can almost walk upright. Apes do not have tails.

## How are humans different from apes?

Humans walk on two feet. We have larger brains and use language.

*Bonobos are close relatives of chimps.*

*Chimpanzees often become good friends.*

# AN APE'S BODY

**An ape's body is perfect for life in the forest. An ape is strong and agile. It can see well under the trees. It has long fingers to gather forest food – and strong jaws to chew it up.**

**Apes have thumbs** on their hands and their feet! The thumb swivels round to face the fingers (or the toes), allowing them to grasp things like twigs and fruit.

A chimpanzee's hand and foot.

A male gorilla

**An ape's longest teeth** are its fangs. Apes often display their fangs to try to frighten away their enemies.

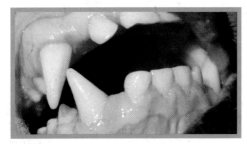

*All apes have sharp teeth called fangs.*

**Legs**
*Strong legs support the gorilla's heavy body.*

**Feet**
*An ape's feet are good at grasping. The big toe is just like a thumb.*

✦ At 50 kg, an adult chimpanzee is lighter than most men, but is about seven times stronger.

✦ Apes have flat fingernails. They do not have claws.

✦ A man's armspan is about 1.5 m. An orang-utan's is a metre wider.

**Jaws**
The jaws have big muscles to chew tough plants.

**Bony ridge**
This bony ridge protects the ape's eyes.

**Eyes**
An ape's eyes face forwards. This helps it to judge distances well in the forest.

**Teeth**
Long, sharp teeth frighten off enemies. Flat teeth are good for chewing.

**Hands**
Strong hands and nimble fingers are good for making nests and gathering food.

**Arms**
Arms are long and strong. They are good for climbing.

**Apes often have** huge pot bellies. This is because they eat a lot of bulky plant food, such as leaves, shoots and stems. The food takes a long time to digest.

## APE WATCH

'I was rounding a turn in the path when a huge orang-utan appeared. He stopped dead in his tracks less than four metres away...I marvelled at how magnificent he looked with his coat blazing orange in the full sunlight.'

Biruté Galdikas-Brindamour,
National Geographic, Oct 1975

# SWINGING ALONG

All apes spend time in the trees. Some swing through the forest canopy. Others climb from branch to branch. But gorillas and chimps prefer to stay on the ground.

**The orang-utan's strong arms** make it a powerful climber. The animal's long, hooked fingers grip the branches tightly – even when it's asleep!

**Gibbons are the fastest movers** in the forest. They run through the treetops on their two hind legs or, more often, just hang from the branches and swing along.

**How gibbons swing through trees**

*An orang-utan hangs from the trees.*

*1. A gibbon hangs from a branch by its left hand...*

When chimps walk on the ground they rest the top part of their body on their knuckles.

## Do apes ever fall?

Yes. When branches snap, apes fall to the ground. Many suffer broken bones.

## Are apes' arms longer than their legs?

Yes. An orang-utan's arms are nearly twice as long.

## When do gorillas learn to walk?

When they are eight to ten months old. But they still like to be carried by their mothers!

**Gorillas and chimps** spend a lot of time on the ground. They walk on all fours, balancing on their knuckles and the soles of their feet. This is called knuckle-walking.

**Gorillas can stand** on two legs – but not for long. They only stand when they want to show off their size, reach up high or carry something in both hands.

2. It swings forward to grasp the next branch with its right hand…

3. Now its left hand lets go and the animal swings forward again.

# A GORILLA'S DAY

**A gorilla group leads a peaceful life. Each day the animals move through the forest. They feed, rest and groom one another, then curl up in a nest for the night.**

*A silverback screams to show he's the boss.*

**A gorilla group** is like a large family. There is an adult male, known as a silverback, one or two younger males, a few adult females, and a handful of youngsters.

**The silverback** is the leader of the group. He decides where the group will feed, when it will move on, and where it will stop and rest.

## APE WATCH

'Peanuts is a showman. He beat his chest; he threw leaves into the air; he swaggered and slapped the leaves around him, and then suddenly he was at my side. He had entertained me, he seemed to say – now it was my turn.'

*Dian Fossey,* National Geographic, *Oct. 1971*

**When there is danger,** the silverback tries to defends the group. He stands upright, beating his chest and baring his teeth. He may even begin to charge. Usually this is just bluff: gorillas rarely attack.

# Daily life

1. Every morning, gorillas move through the forest, feeding as they go.

2. At mid-day, they rest and groom one another.

3. Later, they gather branches to make a nest for the night.

At mid-day, when the sun is hot, gorillas stop for a rest.

**Gorillas groom one another,** picking out the dirt and tiny animals that lodge in their fur. Grooming helps the animals in the group to feel close to one another.

## DID YOU KNOW?

✦ Some gorillas live in tropical rainforests. Others live in mountain forests.

✦ Adult males are known as silverbacks because the fur on their back turns silver with age.

✦ Wild gorillas can live until they are over thirty, but many die young.

# AMBUSH!

*An orang-utan with a mouthful of bananas.*

Most apes are vegetarian. They feed on leaves, stems, fruit and nuts. But one kind of ape has a taste for meat. Chimpanzees hunt monkeys in the forest and kill them in a deadly chase.

**Orang-utans feed** on hundreds of different foods. They love fruit, and seem to know just when a fruit tree is ripening.

**Gorillas use their hands** and teeth with great care to eat their favourite part of a plant: the bark, root, stem, leaves or fruit.

*A gorilla peels the skin off a stem before eating the soft insides.*

**Chimps ambush a monkey**

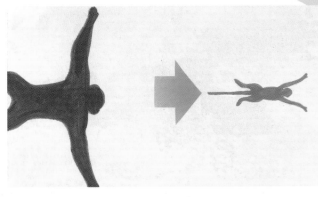

*1. One chimp drives a monkey forwards.*

*2. Others line the route so it can't get away.*

*3. The monkey is ambushed and killed...*

*4. ...and all the chimps feed on its meat.*

## Do apes spend a lot of time feeding?

Yes – five or more hours a day.

## Do apes drink water?

Some do. Orang-utans reach into tree holes and lap water from their hands.

## Do wild apes love bananas?

Most wild apes never see a banana in their lives. They eat hundreds of other foods.

**Chimpanzees in West Africa** hunt monkeys through the forest. The monkeys are light and move faster than the chimps. But the chimps are smart; they use teamwork to trap their prey…

**One chimp chases** a monkey through the forest, while other chimps wait ahead. The monkey panics, and runs straight into an ambush.

# BRAINY APES

**Apes are brainy. They can solve problems and invent new ways of doing things. Many apes are good at communicating. Some have even learned to use tools.**

*By using their faces and touching one another, chimps show how they are feeling.*

**Chimpanzees communicate well** with each other – by hugging, patting, grunting, calling and using lots of different expressions. Every chimp knows how the others feel. This helps them all to get on.

## APE WATCH

'In the wild, gorillas sing. They especially like to sing after a fierce thunderstorm has ended, and the rainforest air smells sweet...Their singing certainly sounds as if it is coming from a happy animal.'

*From* The Singing Gorilla
*by George Page*

**Common chimp expressions**

*Sad*

*Playful*

*Anxious*

Scientists have taught sign language to some chimps and gorillas. The animals will never be able to speak, because they can't make the right kinds of sound.

Chimps have learned to use tools. They use heavy stones to break open nuts.

Chimps use twigs to get termites out of their nests. They poke the twig through a hole in the nest and 'fish' around for the tasty insects inside.

*Termite nests are rock hard. This chimp is fishing out termites with a twig.*

# BABY APE

Baby apes grow up slowly. They have a lot to learn: how to climb, find food and make a nest. They must also learn how to behave properly with their elders.

*A gorilla with her tiny ten-day-old baby.*

**A female orang-utan** has one baby at a time. She is its most important teacher. The baby stays close to her for five or more years before going off to live on its own.

**Ape mothers** spend a lot of time cradling their young. In time, they let other females touch the baby, too. Watching and cuddling new infants is one way that female apes learn to be mothers.

**A growing orang-utan**

## APE WATCH

'I defy anyone who knows anything about children to watch a small chimpanzee and not realize...that the chimp has exactly the same feelings and fears as human infants.'

*Jane Goodall, quoted in* The Singing Gorilla *by George Page*

*1. A baby orang-utan is tiny when it is born.*

*As they play, young chimps learn when to stand up for themselves and when to give way.*

**Baby chimps play** for hours every day, chasing and fighting one another. Playing helps the animals grow quicker and stronger. Adults often play with them, too.

## How heavy is a newborn gorilla?

It weighs about 1.5 kg – about half the weight of a human baby.

## Is the silverback a good father?

Yes. He watches and protects his baby, and lets it play on his back.

## Does a baby orang-utan play with another?

No. It lives alone with its mother.

**Baby gorillas** have a white tuft of hair on their bottom. This stands out in the shady forest and helps their mothers to keep an eye on them.

2. **For the first few months, it clings to its mother.**

3. *Then it starts to climb nearby trees.*

# APES IN DANGER

**Great apes face a life of danger. They are sold as pets and hunted for their meat. Now their forest habitats are disappearing. Could apes soon become extinct?**

**Thousands of great apes** are killed every year. Some are shot by farmers for stealing fruit. Others are killed by hunters for their meat.

**Great apes breed** very slowly. If more apes die than are born each year, these animals will become extinct.

*A dead mountain gorilla. Only about 500 of these gorillas survive.*

*A young orang-utan orphan.*

## APE WATCH

'From a sack, the owner of the carcass suddenly took out the gorilla's huge black hand, which had been cut off at the wrist. Its fingers were still flexible as passers-by…inspected the meat. It looked so human…'

The Slaughter of the Apes *by Garry Richardson*

**Female apes** are often killed so that their young can be sold as pets. Baby apes look cute, but they soon grow big. Because they have never learned to fend for themselves, they cannot be returned to the wild.

**The orang-utan's habitat** is shrinking. The rainforest is being cut down for timber and to make room for ranches and farms. The great ape is struggling to survive.

*Food and shelter are disappearing as the south-east Asian rainforests are cut down.*

## DID YOU KNOW?

✦ Each year, in the Congo alone, up to 600 gorillas and 3,000 chimps are killed for their meat.

✦ Local hunters earn a month's wages for every gorilla they kill.

✦ Apes are killed so their meat can be sold at high prices to rich people.

# HELPING APES

Apes are a great tourist attraction.

Many people are helping apes. Scientists are learning about them. Conservationists are trying to protect them. Tourists are visiting them.

**Tourists help gorillas** and orang-utans by paying to see them in the wild. The money they bring in is used to pay for extra wardens, who work to protect the apes.

In sanctuaries, apes get used to humans and the non-stop supply of food.

**Ape orphans** live in sanctuaries. At first they are fed on milk and bananas. Later, as they grow bigger, food is left for them deeper in the forest. But few return to the wild.

*Park wardens have identity cards for the gorillas on their patch.*

**In many countries,** apes live in national parks where hunting is banned. Park wardens patrol the parks, watching for poachers. It is a dangerous job. Some poachers have killed wardens rather than face arrest.

**Some scientists** spend their working lives watching and studying apes. Their work teaches us more about the animals and their way of life.

## DID YOU KNOW?

✦ Scientists who study apes in the wild learn to move and grunt like an ape.

✦ In sanctuaries, orang-utans play together in gangs; this never happens in the wild.

✦ Tourists who want to see gorillas have to put up with long walks, mosquitoes and rain!

# APES QUIZ

Can you find the right answers to these questions? They can all be found somewhere in this book. Check your answers on page 29.

1. How many kinds of ape are there?
a 5
b 15
c 50

2. Which of these animals are primates?
a Cats
b Zebras
c Monkeys

3. Why do apes have strong jaws?
a To chew plants
b To pull down branches
c To bite one another

4. What is special about apes' thumbs?
a They have long fingernails
b They bend backwards
c They can swivel round to face the fingers

5. Which is the fastest ape in the forest?
a The orang-utan
b The gibbon
c The chimpanzee

6. Which ape prefers to stay on the ground?
a The gorilla
b The orang-utan
c The gibbon

**7.** **What name is given to the leader of a gorilla group?**
a The boss
b The silverback
c Prime ape

**8.** **What do gorillas do at mid-day?**
a They beat their chests
b They travel through the forest
c They rest

**9.** **Which ape hunts and kills monkeys?**
a The gibbon
b The chimpanzee
c The orang-utan

**10.** **Where do orang-utans find water?**
a In tree holes
b In ponds
c Inside plants

**11.** **How do chimps use heavy stones?**
a As nutcrackers
b As weapons
c As bricks

**12.** **What do chimps use to catch termites?**
a A banana
b A heavy stone
c A long twig

**13.** **When does a young orang-utan leave its mother?**
a After a year
b After five years
c Never

**14.** **What makes baby gorillas easy to spot?**
a Their pink skin
b The white tuft of hair on their bottom
c Their red fur

**15.** **How many mountain gorillas live in the wild?**
a About 500
b About 5,000
c About 50,000

**16.** **How are tourists helping great apes?**
a They watch for poachers
b They bring in a lot of money
c They feed the young ape orphans

27

# GLOSSARY

**agile** Quick-moving and active.

**ambush** To lie in wait and make a surprise attack.

**canopy** The highest leaves and branches in a forest.

**carcass** A dead body.

**communicate** To share information and feelings with another animal or person.

**conservationist** A person who wants to protect wildlife and help it to survive.

**digest** To break down food in the body.

**extinct** Died out – no longer living anywhere in the world.

**fang** A very long, pointed tooth.

**grasslands** Dry areas where there are grasses but very few trees.

**knuckle-walking** A way of walking practised by gorillas and chimps. They rest on the soles of their feet and carry their weight on their knuckles.

**national park** A piece of land that has been set aside for the protection of wild animals.

**orphan** A young animal whose mother has died.

**poacher** Someone who catches animals that are protected by law.

**primates** A group of animals that includes monkeys, apes and humans.

**sanctuary** A safe place where young apes are cared for.

**silverback** An adult male gorilla.

**termite** An ant-like insect that lives in large groups inside a nest.

**warden** A person who cares for animals in a sanctuary or national park.

# FINDING OUT MORE

## Books

*Gorilla* by Ian Redmond (Dorling Kindersley, 1995)

*Gorillas* by Patricia Miller-Schroeder (A & C Black, 1999)

*The Great Apes* by Michael Leach (Blandford, 1997)

*I Didn't Know that Chimps Use Tools* by Claire Llewellyn (Aladdin Books, 1999)

## Websites

Here are some places to start.

www.4apes.com
The ape alliance, a group of wildlife charities that help primates.

www.kilimanjaro.com/wspa/wspa.htm
Website of the World Society for the Protection of Animals. Information about the dangers apes face.

www.orangutans-sos.org
Sumatran orang-utan society.

www.primates.net
A photographer's pictures of great apes and the stories behind them, with links to other websites.

www.janegoodall.org
Jane Goodall is one of the world's leading experts on chimpanzees.

www.primates-online.com
Website of the Primate Conservation and Welfare Society.

www.gorillafund.org/
The website of the Dian Fossey Gorilla Fund International. Dian Fossey was a leading expert on mountain gorillas.

www.orangutan.org/movie.html
A short film about the danger to orang-utans with links to a general website.

## Places to visit

You can visit great apes at zoos in Atherstone, Belfast, Blackpool, Bristol, Chester, Colchester, Colwyn Bay, Dunstable, Edinburgh, Jersey, Kessingland, London, Paignton and Southport.

## Answers to quiz

| | | | |
|---|---|---|---|
| 1 a | 5 b | 9 b | 13 b |
| 2 c | 6 a | 10 a | 14 b |
| 3 a | 7 b | 11 a | 15 a |
| 4 c | 8 c | 12 c | 16 b |

 # INDEX

Page numbers in **bold** mean there is a picture on the page.

## A
arms 11, **11**, 12, **12**, 13, **13**

## B
babies 20, **20**, 21, **21**, 23, **23**, 24
body 10, **10**, 11, **11**
bonobos 8, 9, **9**

## C
chimpanzees 8, **9**, 9, **10**, 11, 13, **13**, 16, 17, **17**, 18, **18**, 19, **19**, 20, 21, **21**, **24**
communication 18, **18**, 19
conservationists 24

## D
dangers to apes 22, 23
drinking 17

## F
feet 10, **10**
food 11, 16, **16**, 17, **17**, 24

## G
gibbons 8, 9, 12, **12**, 13

gorillas 8, **8**, 9, **10**, **11**, 13, 14, **14**, 15, **15**, 16, **16**, 18, 19, **20**, 21, **22**, 23, 24, 25, **25**
grooming 15, **15**
groups, ape 9, 14, 15, **15**

## H
hands 10, **10**, 11
hunting apes 22, **22**, 23, 25
hunting by apes 16, 17, **17**

## K
knuckle-walking 13, **13**

## M
movement 12, **12**, 13, **13**

## N
national parks 25

## O
orang-utans 8, **8**, 9, 11, 12, **12**, 13, 16, **16**, 17, 19, 20, **20**, 21, **21**, 23, **23**, 24, **24**
orphan apes 23, 24

## P
play 21, **21**
poachers 25
pot bellies 10, 11
primates 8, 9

## R
rainforests 9, 23, **23**
resting **15**

## S
sanctuaries 24, **24**
scientists 24, 25
sign language 19
silverback 14, **14**, 15, 21

## T
teeth 10, **10**
thumbs 10, **10**
tool use 19, **19**
tourists 24, **24**, 25

## W
wardens 24, 25, **25**

**Picture acknowledgements**
Bruce Coleman 18, (Gerald S. Cubitt) 23 (below); Corbis (Yann Arthus-Bertrand) 10 (below), (Carmen Redondo) 16 (below); Getty Images (Clayton Fogle) *Cover*, (Manoj Shah) 8 (right), (Renee Lynn) 12, (Manoj Shah) 16 (above), (Tim Davis) 19, (James Martin) 24 (above); NHPA (Martin Harvey) 10 (above), (Christophe Ratier) 13, (Mark Bowler) 20, (Nigel J. Dennis) 21, (Martin Harvey) 24 (below), (Martin Harvey) 25; OSF (Konrad Wothe) 15; Robert Harding (Minden Pictures) 9 (left), (L. Bloom) 14; Still Pictures (Fritz Polking) 8 (left), (Robert Henno) 9 (right), (Michael Gunther) 22, (Tantyo Bangun) 23 (above).

**Other acknowledgements**
*The Singing Gorilla*, quoted on pages 18 and 20, is published by Hodder Headline. *Slaughter of the Apes*, quoted on pages 23, is from the World Society for the Protection of Animals website.